HER MAJESTY QUEEN ELIZABETH THE

QUEEN MOTHER

WOMAN OF THE CENTURY

HUGH MASSINGBERD

MACMILLAN

The Daily Telegraph

The Daily Telegraph

First published 1999 by Macmillan, an imprint of Macmillan Publishers Ltd
25 Eccleston Place, London SW1W 9NF
Associated companies throughout the world

ISBN 0333 75980 X

ENDPAPER: *Queen Elizabeth with her daughters, Princess Elizabeth and Princess Margaret, 1941.*
FRONTISPIECE: *The Coronation group at Buckingham Palace, May 12 1937.* ABOVE: *Brave faces at the time of
the Abdication, 1936.* RIGHT: *A romantic portrait of the Queen Consort by Cecil Beaton, 1948.*

To Mr & Mrs
Brearton Robertson
Lawa Booth

CONTENTS

THE WAR YEARS

1939 - 1945

PEACE COMES

1946 - 1959

AMONGST THE STARS

TOP OF THE BILL

THE JUBILEE AND BEYOND

1977 - 1999

QUEEN MOTHER

1900

The infant Elizabeth Bowes-Lyon, youngest daughter of Lord and Lady Glamis, in her perambulator at St Paul's Walden Bury, the family's Hertfordshire home near Hitchin, with her paternal grandmother, the Countess of Strathmore. Lady Strathmore, the wife of the 13th Earl, was formerly Frances Smith from a City banking family; her husband died in 1904. Much of Elizabeth's childhood was spent at St Paul's.

THE life story of Her Majesty Queen Elizabeth The Queen Mother is, in many ways, the history of the 20th century. As Elizabeth Bowes-Lyon, she was born with the century, in 1900, into the *ancien regime* of aristocratic privilege and *noblesse oblige* still presided over by Queen Victoria, Empress of India. The Great War – which was to have such a decisive effect on her character, shaping her philosophy of rising above gloom and disaster – broke out on Lady Elizabeth's 14th birthday. Afterwards her "justly famous charm" (in the words of the Duchess of Windsor, not one of her admirers) as a dainty Duchess of York helped transform the appeal of the Royal House of Windsor from admiration and respect to warmth and love; her effervescent British blood enlivened a stuffy Germanic dynasty which for centuries had chosen its brides from the continent. Then, as the maternal, plucky and resolute Queen Elizabeth, she enabled her husband King George VI and the Monarchy to sail serenely over the shock of the Abdication of King Edward VIII. During the Second World War she came to symbolise the heroism of the Home Front; indeed she became the war's last surviving star. Ultimately, after her husband's death in 1952, she achieved her apotheosis as "the Queen Mum" – "the great mother figure and nanny to us all", as Sir Cecil Beaton, her principal iconographer, described her.

As a 20th-century icon and survivor, the Queen Mother's significance can hardly be exaggerated. She was the first Queen since Catherine Parr (Henry VIII's sixth bride) not to have been of royal birth; she was the first Queen Mother to be the parent of a reigning Queen; she was the last Empress of India. As each year passed, more records accrued to her longevity: by 1998, for instance, she had been a member of the Royal Family for 75 years and she also overtook Princess Alice, Countess of Athlone, Queen Victoria's last surviving granddaughter (who died in 1981, aged 97 years and 313 days) to become the oldest-ever member of the Royal Family.

Yet symbolism and statistics signify little compared with the Queen Mother's essentially human qualities. And these too have tended to be obscured by the cosy, clichéd image of "the Queen Mum" – an appellation almost invariably accompanied by the sentimental formula, "Gawd, bless 'er!" Certainly the familiar vision of the Queen Mother, a radiant picture in tulle and flowery hats, her head slightly to one side as she waves winsomely, is by no means the whole story. It could be said that the "Queen Mum" persona developed more than a hint of self-parody over the years. One revealing anecdote concerns the time she went to see her son-in-law the Earl of Snowdon's restored cottage in Sussex. Invited to perform the "opening ceremony", she proceeded to give a facetious imitation of the traditional "Queen Mum Show", sending herself up mercilessly.

An enthusiastic mimic, she has always loved charades, practical jokes and such party games as "Parade", in which she would pretend to "review" other guests marching past. At her 90th birthday celebrations on

1901

She had been christened "Elizabeth Angela Marguerite" at All Saints, St Paul's Walden Bury, the previous autumn. The next year she acquired a baby brother, David. As they were so much younger than their siblings, their mother nicknamed them "The Two Benjamins", an allusion to the Biblical story of Jacob's youngest son.

Horse Guards, where all manner of livestock and strangely attired "showbiz" luminaries paraded past her, Her Majesty was manifestly in her element.

Some have gone so far as to portray Queen Elizabeth (to use the style by which she has continued to be known within her close circle) as a cosseted, "camp" actress. Her least obliging biographer, Penelope Mortimer, observed that "the smiles, the words, the applause – were second nature to her". Pursuing the theatrical analogy through the stages of her life, the Queen Mother is variously depicted as the "Pollyanna" of Glamis, enchanting the wounded soldiers recuperating in her ancestral castle during the First World War, the "Faerie Queene" of the Thirties, an exalted "Mrs Miniver" in the Second World War and the jolly old "Queen Gran" of *Spitting Image*. Mrs Mortimer brought the curtain down on her remarkably catty study with the Queen Mother's supposedly favourite scene from her friend Sir Noel Coward's play *Private Lives*: "Let's be superficial and pity the poor Philosophers. Let's blow trumpets and squeakers, and enjoy the party as much as we can, like small, quite idiotic schoolchildren. Let's savour the delights of the moment."

A more sympathetic biographer, Elizabeth Longford, maintained that Her Majesty's splendid act was in no sense artificial. The late Lord David Cecil, a childhood friend, pointed out that "her sense of duty and patriotism are helped by her dramatic sense. She thinks she ought to wave and give pleasure. And she is able to perform these feelings to the public."

For my part, I prefer to draw an analogy not with Coward but with another of Her Majesty's favourite writers, P.G. Wodehouse. It is a sound rule to divide the world up into Wodehousians (good eggs, with a sense of humour) and non-Wodehousians (po-faced pills like the politicians who delayed his knighthood on account of some innocent, if ill-judged, broadcasts during the Second World War). It was typical of Her Majesty, when the honour finally came through, to offer to fly out to America to confer the accolade on the great humorist. Indeed, she herself appeared by implication in *The Mating Season*. Her *alter ego* deals tactfully with an Irish guest at Buckingham Palace who has half-a-dozen helpings of Mulligatawny under the impression that there will be no further courses.

It has always been easy to detect more than a touch of the Master's sparky, bubbly, occasionally steely heroines such as "Bobbie" Wickham or "Stiffy" Byng – "spirited damsels, human ticking bombs", as Wodehouse calls them – in the Queen Mother's personality. In short, the key to Her Majesty's character has been her Wodehousian sense of fun. "Isn't this fun?" she would say during her remorseless round of official engagements. Or, in response to some wild proposal: "What fun! *Do* let's do it."

Although born in the reign of Queen Victoria she enjoyed the innovations and inventions of her century, entering with unquenchable gaiety into new adventures and listening to new ideas, while never renouncing good old-fashioned virtues and principles. Early in her widowhood, for example, she was buzzing around Europe in the new Comet jet airliner and flying in a helicopter. She continued to travel extensively well into her 10th decade – fulfilling a long-held ambition to see Venice and visiting Canada so often that there was talk of her settling there. She carried on gardening, fishing and racing in often unspeakable weather conditions.

To see Her Majesty attending one of her beloved National Hunt race-meetings at Cheltenham, Sandown Park or Newbury has been to witness an exercise in infectiously relaxed style. Together with her faithful bachelor entourage – such as the late Sir Martin "Each-Way" Gilliat – would be rugs, a thermos of champagne and perhaps a flask of whisky. The question as to what Her Majesty's capacious handbag might contain was memorably answered during one of her regular regimental visits when the bag fell on to the parade ground and broke open to reveal a cascade of chocolate violet creams.

Appropriately enough, Her Majesty's birthday in early August used to coincide with the opening of the National Hunt season. She became

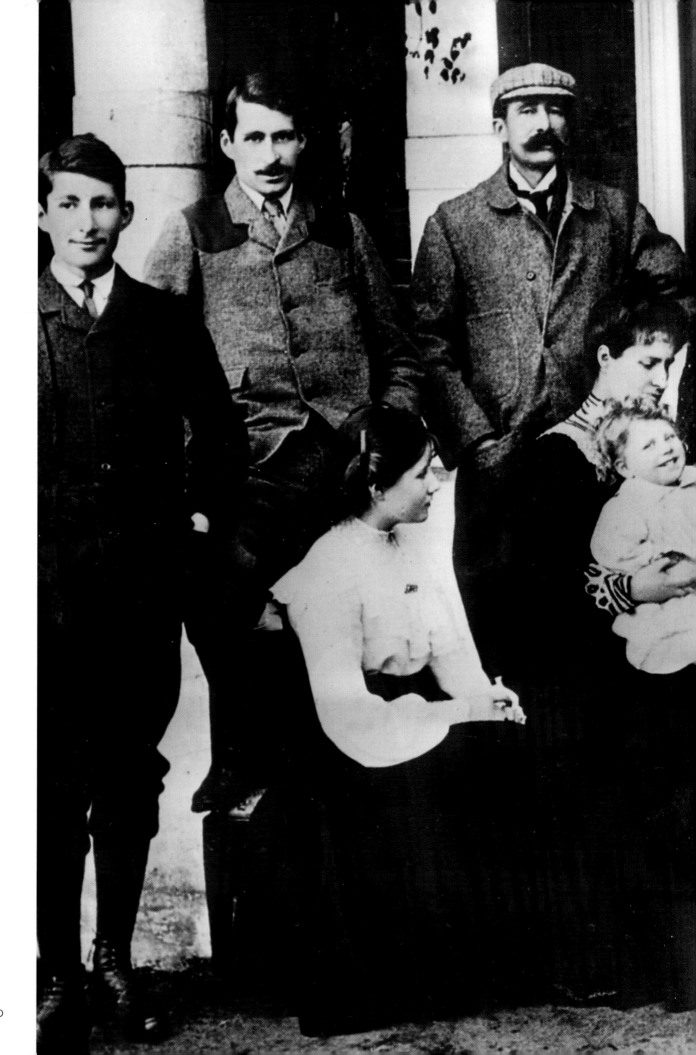

A Glamis family group taken in the year that Elizabeth's baby brother, David, was born. Altogether Lord and Lady Glamis had 10 children, but the eldest, Violet, born in 1882, had died of diphtheria in 1893. From left to right: Fergus (1889-1915); Jock (1886-1920); Rose, later Countess Granville (1890-1967); Lord Glamis, later 14th Earl of Strathmore (died 1944); Lady Glamis, later Countess of Strathmore (died 1938) holding David; Mary ("May"), later Lady Elphinstone (1883-1961); Elizabeth; Michael (1893-1953); Patrick, later 15th Earl of Strathmore (1884-1949); and Alec (1887-1911).

1904

"The Two Benjamins" in the year that their father, Lord Glamis, succeeded to the Earldom of Strathmore and Kinghorne, the ancestral seat of Glamis Castle and the family estates and was also appointed Lord-Lieutenant of Angus. On her father's succession to the Earldom, Elizabeth's style of address altered from being "the Honourable Elizabeth Bowes-Lyon" to "Lady Elizabeth Bowes-Lyon". Her brother David, who was her great childhood companion, lived in later life at St Paul's Walden Bury, served as Lord-Lieutenant of Hertfordshire and was appointed a Knight Commander of the Royal Victorian Order before his death in 1961.

celebrated for enjoying a flutter: Clarence House, her London home, was early equipped with a bookies' blower to give her direct access to the results. As one racing journalist remarked: "If there is a shorter cut to a bloody nose in Tattersall's than to criticise the Queen Mum in any way, I do not know it."

And yet, as her father-in-law, King George V – a gruff character whom she utterly enchanted – observed, it would be horrible if she were perfect. The only fault that this nautical martinet found in his daughter-in-law was her tendency to be late – a breach of the proverbial politeness of princes.

The truth is that the sentiment and gush – of which, inevitably, we have had a surfeit as "the Queen Mum" has passed ever more milestones – has obscured the essential Queen Elizabeth. As another of her racecourse companions, the late Lord Wyatt of Weeford (Woodrow Wyatt), pointed out, Her Majesty was "not all sugar. She can be a little acid when necessary."

Let no one doubt that there has always been a filament of tough Scottish steel within the "English Rose" flowery exterior. "For someone so unaggressive," said Lord David Cecil, "she has a very strong personality – she could be formidable."

Of all the misconceptions about "the Queen Mum", the most absurd is that of the "mumsy", middle-class, suburban hausfrau. Long before she married the future King George VI, her "blood family" (to borrow the terminology of Earl Spencer in his address at the funeral of his sister, Diana Princess of Wales), the Bowes-Lyons, Earls of Strathmore and Kinghorne, were one of the most august of the Great Families of Scotland. Their family seat, Glamis, is everyone's idea of a Scottish castle, with its massive tower and cluster of pointed turrets. Dating mostly from the 15th to 17th centuries, it incorporates fragments of a hunting lodge of the medieval Scots Kings, to whom it belonged until King Robert II granted it to his son-in-law, Sir John Lyon ("The White Lyon") in 1372.

The castle and lands reverted to the Crown for a period in the 16th century when it was seized by King James V at the same time as he had the widowed Lady Glamis burned at the stake in Edinburgh on a trumped-up charge of practising sorcery. Reputed to be the most haunted castle in Scotland, Glamis's ghosts are traditionally said to include "Earl Beardie", the "White Lady", the "Tongueless Woman" and the legendary, if now not mentioned "Monster of Glamis" (supposedly a hairy, egg-like creature).

In the 17th century the Lyons, Lords Glamis, obtained the Earldom of Strathmore. The family name became Bowes-Lyon after the Strathmores heir inherited the estates of the coal-rich Durham family of Bowes, whose heiress married the 9th Earl of Strathmore in 1767.

The "Princess" (as she was prophetically known as a child) was not born at Glamis or indeed (as it was incorrectly registered at the time) at her parents' home in Hertfordshire, St Pauls Walden Bury, on August 4 1900. The birth actually took place in London, though precisely where remains unidentified – there is a theory that it occurred in a horse-drawn ambulance.

The baby girl was baptised "Elizabeth Angela Marguerite". She was the youngest daughter and ninth child of Lord Glamis, eldest son and heir of the 13th Earl of Strathmore and Kinghorne and his wife, the former Nina Cecilia ("Celia") Cavendish-Bentinck, a clergyman's daughter and a cousin of the Duke of Portland (half-brother of the eccentric Bloomsbury hostess, Lady Ottoline Morrell). In 1902 young Elizabeth acquired a baby brother, David. Lady Glamis nicknamed her two youngest children, who were more than a decade junior to their nearest siblings, "my two Benjamins", after the Biblical story of Jacob's youngest son.

In 1904 Lord Glamis's father died and he succeeded as the 14th Earl of Strathmore, whereupon Elizabeth, previously known by courtesy "the Honourable", became styled "Lady Elizabeth". Her mother took a special interest in educating her daughters at home with the help of governesses (as was then the practice for girls); particular emphasis was placed on foreign languages and English Literature.

1907

OPPOSITE: *Lady Elizabeth Bowes-Lyon (nicknamed "Princess" in her family) at the age when she had her hand read by a palmist at a fête. "She says I'm going to be a Queen when I grow up!" she reported to her French governess Mlle ("Madé") Lang. "Isn't it silly?"*

The Strathmores had a London house in St James's Square from where Lady Elizabeth would venture out to children's parties. At one of these occasions, in 1905, Lady Elizabeth is supposed to have sat next to her future husband, Prince Albert, second son of the then Prince of Wales and grandson of the reigning King Edward VII. The story goes that they discussed her Shetland pony, Bobs, and her bullfinch, Bobby. After tea, the Prince is supposed to have said, "Don't go away"; and Lady Elizabeth to have replied, "I won't, if you want me to stay." Neither later recalled this doubtless romanticised encounter.

Another attractive myth of Lady Elizabeth's early years was the reading of her palm at a fête in 1907. "She says I'm going to be Queen when I grow up!" she allegedly reported back to her French governess, "Madé" Lang. "Isn't it silly?" Mlle Lang was later succeeded by a German governess, Fraulein Kuebler, who departed on the outbreak of war in 1914.

Lady Elizabeth spent most of the First World War at Glamis, which was transformed by her mother, Lady Strathmore, into a convalescent home for wounded soldiers. It was in this slightly surreal atmosphere that Lady Elizabeth blossomed from a sweet and sometimes mischievous adolescent into a strikingly vivacious and attractive debutante. Although news from the Front was distressingly bleak – her brother Fergus was killed at Loos, her brother Michael (wrongly) reported dead, along with many of their friends and contemporaries – Lady Elizabeth energetically took on the role of cheering up her charges at Glamis. Some sheet music on the piano in the Castle's billiard room epitomises her approach to life: "Just Snap Your Fingers At Dull Care".

She was celebrated for playing pranks on the wounded soldiers. Her brother David, in dowagerish "drag", would be solemnly escorted round the wards. "Yip I Addy I Ay" was substituted for Handel as the harmonium voluntary at Sunday service in the chapel. The men were bewitched by her antics. "May you be hung, drawn and quartered," inscribed one military wag in Lady Elizabeth's autograph book. "Yes, hung in diamonds, drawn in coach-and-four and quartered in the best house in the land."

In 1919 the Strathmores launched their pretty little (5ft 2ins) daughter in Society with a coming-out ball. Many young men were smitten by her charms, notably James Stuart (later 1st Viscount Stuart of Findhorn) – and her old children's party companion, Prince Albert, who was created Duke of York in 1920. That year the new Duke came over to Glamis from the royal estate of Balmoral and on a visit in 1921 he wrote to his mother, Queen Mary: "It is delightful here & Elizabeth is very kind to me. The more I see of her the more I like her."

In 1922 Lady Elizabeth Bowes-Lyon became a national celebrity as a bridesmaid to the Duke's sister, Princess Mary, with whom she shared an interest in Girl Guiding. Speculation was already growing that she might marry the Duke of York, or even the Prince of Wales (though, to say the least, he never fell under the spell of "Cookie", as he unkindly called her). But "Bertie's" courtship was not going smoothly. Queen Mary's canny confidante the Countess of Airlie noted that Lady Elizabeth was "frankly doubtful, uncertain of her feelings and afraid of the public life which would be asked of her as the King's daughter-in-law". Learning of his second son's intentions, King George V observed: "You'll be a lucky fellow if she accepts you."

Finally, she did, in January 1923 during a walk through the woods at St Paul's Walden Bury. "I am not sure," she later commented, "that I wasn't the most surprised of the two." Using a pre-arranged code, the Duke of York telegraphed his delighted parents at Sandringham: "ALL RIGHT. BERTIE."

It was to be the first time a Briton had married someone close to the British Throne since the mid-17th century when Lady Anne Hyde, daughter of the Earl of Clarendon (who, incidentally, considered her to be "a presumptuous strumpet") married an earlier Duke of York (later King James II). But this break with precedent proved universally popular,

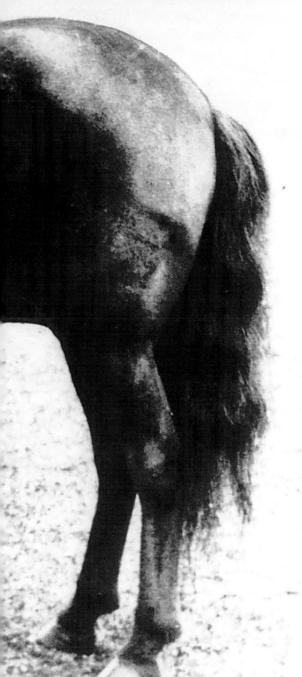

1909

LEFT: *Lady Elizabeth riding side-saddle on her faithful Shetland pony Bobs at St Paul's Walden Bury. She had learnt to ride at the age of three. Bobs was supposedly a topic of conversation – along with her bullfinch, Bobby – when she first met her future husband, Prince Albert (second son of the then Prince of Wales and grandson of the reigning monarch, King Edward VII) at a children's party at Montagu House in London in 1905. After tea the Prince is supposed to have said, "Don't go away,"* and Lady Elizabeth to have replied, *"I won't if you want me to stay." Neither later recalled this encounter or exchange.*

BELOW: *The Two Benjamins in their dancing outfits, in which their mother, Lady Strathmore, would cajole them to perform at Glamis entertainments. "Princess" Elizabeth's pink and silver brocade dress was copied by Lady Strathmore from a painting by Velasquez; David's "dressing-up" attire was a jester's costume (the Lyons were said to be the last family in Scotland to maintain a jester on the payroll).*

1912

A wistful study of Lady Elizabeth as her childhood comes to an end. The previous year her brother Alec had died of a brain tumour after being hit on the head by a cricket ball; and in the autumn of 1912 her brother David, the younger of "The Two Benjamins" was sent away to private school at Broadstairs. "I miss him horribly," says Lady Elizabeth, who herself spends two terms at the Misses Birtwhistle's day school in Sloane Street, London, after "Madé", her governess, leaves to get married.

1914

OPPOSITE: *Fast maturing into a young woman, Lady Elizabeth's 14th birthday falls on the same day that war is declared with Germany. That evening she goes to a show at the Coliseum Theatre starring Charles Hawtrey. Her new German governess, Fraulein Kuebler, departs. Soon afterwards the Strathmores move up to Glamis, which is converted into a convalescent hospital for wounded soldiers.*

particularly in the wake of the "Kaiser's War". Doubtless plenty of Scots even considered that Lady Elizabeth was rather marrying beneath her in becoming the wife of the second son of a Hanoverian dynasty.

In eventually deciding to accept the awkward, stammering and insecure Prince Bertie's persistent proposals, Lady Elizabeth was assuredly doing that dynasty an incalculable favour. Apart from her personal attributes, she had the great advantage of not being born "royal". As an unselfconscious young Scottish aristocrat she was secure in her position and content to be herself. Not for her the suffocating stuffiness and cumbersome protocol of Teutonic royalty.

As well as bolstering her husband's confidence and bringing out his sterling qualities that few had recognised (he was, as Lady Strathmore remarked, a man who would be "made or marred by his wife"), the new Duchess of York proceeded to humanise the stiff and shy Royal Family. "Elizabeth is so charming, so pretty & engaging & natural," noted Queen Mary. Employing the classic feminine wiles, the "Smiling Duchess" (as she became known) literally flirted her way into the nation's heart. During a visit to Northern Ireland in 1924, the Duke of York reported to his father: "Elizabeth has been marvellous as usual and the people simply love her already. I am very lucky indeed to have her to help me as she knows exactly what to do and say to all the people we meet."

It was the same story everywhere "the Little Duchess" went, though the six-month absence, on a tour of the Empire in 1927, from her baby daughter, Princess Elizabeth, must have been hard to bear. In 1930 the Duchess had another daughter, Princess Margaret, born at Glamis – the first royal birth to take place in Scotland since 1602, and also the last occasion that the Home Secretary had to be present for the delivery.

In the first half of the 1930s the Yorks had the much-prized opportunity to lead a fairly "normal" family life. During this all too brief "golden age" the weeks were spent at No.145 Piccadilly and the weekends at Royal Lodge, Windsor, where the Duke and Duchess created a fine rose and rhododendron garden and the two little Princesses played in their tiny thatched cottage, *Y Bwthyn Bach*, a present from the people of Wales. Like her mother before her, the Duchess of York took a keen interest in her daughter's education – stressing the importance of obedience to God, response to duty and thoughtfulness to others, as well as of languages.

Nothing evokes the cosiness of "us four"(as the Duke of York fondly envisaged his family) better than James Gunn's painting, *Conversation Piece at Royal Lodge*. We see the family at tea: the mother preparing to pour from the pot, the tweed-clad father, the clean-cut daughters, the solitary fruit cake, the corgi snoozing on the carpet.

The Empire was enchanted. Unfortunately, though, the contrast between this sort of idyllic domestic scene and the raffish behaviour of the woefully immature Prince of Wales at Fort Belvedere nearby became all too apparent. Matters came to a head after the death of King George V in 1936 – the disastrous year of "the Three Kings".

The errant Edward VIII kept his brother and heir presumptive in the dark about his plans to marry Mrs Simpson, an American divorcée. The Yorks had no foreknowledge of the fate that was to be thrust upon them; they naturally had no desire to see the new King abdicate nor any ambition to succeed. Yet suddenly the Duchess of York was confronted with Mrs Simpson as her hostess at Balmoral in September 1936. She unmistakably registered her disapproval.

The Duke of York did not receive an explanation from his elusive brother until only a few days before the Abdication. The Duchess took to her bed, and so missed the grisly gathering following the Abdication broadcast. "That last family dinner party was too awful," she said many years later. "Thank goodness I had 'flu and couldn't go."

When it came to the crunch, though, the new Queen Consort, Elizabeth, was not lacking in courage. "We must take what is coming," she remarked to the Princesses' governess, "and make the best of it." To the Archbishop of Canterbury, Dr Cosmo Lang, Queen Elizabeth wrote: "I can hardly

believe that we have been called to this tremendous task and (I am writing to you quite intimately) the curious thing is that we are not afraid."

Queen Elizabeth's lack of fear and remarkable calmness in the face of adversity played a key role in stabilising the situation. Thanks largely to her, the Monarchy not only survived the Abdication crisis but emerged from it stronger than ever. The Coronation of May 12 1937 was greeted with enormous enthusiasm. A colour film of the ceremony in Westminster Abbey, featuring the little Princesses in their miniature coronets, proved a great hit all round the Empire. On three successive nights insistent crowds brought the new King – now George VI – and his Queen Consort, Elizabeth, out on to the balcony. The nightmare of the Abdication was forgotten.

The "honeymoon" period that followed for the King and Queen was all too brief as war clouds gathered once more over Europe. Yet, together with her husband, Queen Elizabeth enjoyed two triumphant tours: first to France in 1938, where her full-length white mourning dresses (worn to mark the death of her mother) captivated the Parisians with their *chic*; and then, in 1939, to North America. During six weeks in Canada the King and Queen covered 4,500 miles from coast to coast. Queen Elizabeth enraptured the Canadians. Asked whether she was Scottish or English, she replied: "Since we reached Quebec, I've been a Canadian." As the Governor-General, Lord Tweedsmuir (otherwise John Buchan, the author), shrewdly noted, the Queen "has a perfect genius for the right kind of publicity". The success of the visit surely ensured the Dominion's full-blooded support for the Allied cause in the Second World War.

Similarly the impact made by the ensuing tour of the United States – the first time a reigning British sovereign had set foot on American soil – was to have lasting significance. In Washington the King and Queen were entertained by President Roosevelt, who took them to Mount Vernon, home of the Queen's second cousin six times removed, George Washington. "The King's tour," wrote one American journalist, "is the Queen's triumph."

With hindsight it can be said that the only time the new King put a foot wrong was by inviting the Prime Minister, Neville Chamberlain, to share the balcony at Buckingham Palace with the Queen and himself after the shoddy Munich "agreement" with Hitler which was supposed to ensure "peace in our time". This constitutional blunder could well have damaged relations with Chamberlain's successor, Winston Churchill (whose support for Edward VIII in the Abdication crisis had hardly endeared him to the King and Queen), but, like everyone else, Britain's wartime leader soon fell victim to Queen Elizabeth's charm. "Your Majesties," he told the King and Queen in the dark days of 1940 when Britain stood alone, "are more deeply loved by all classes of your subjects than were any of the Princes of the past."

Queen Elizabeth became Commander-in-Chief of the Women's Royal Naval Service, the Auxiliary Territorial Service and the Women's Auxiliary Air Force (though she decided not to wear uniform), and also took a special interest in the facilities for evacuated mothers and children. As to the proposal to evacuate her own daughters to North America, the Queen was adamant: "The children could not go without me. I won't leave the King, and of course the King will never leave."

A popular song of the day was "The King is Still in London" and the boost for morale in having the King and Queen with the heart of their people in Buckingham Palace (where they insisted on observing the rules of austerity) was immense. And when the palace was bombed in September 1940, Queen Elizabeth famously remarked to a policeman: "Now I can look the East End in the face." Her visits to the worst bombed-out areas in the country during the Blitz were inspirational. As Churchill wrote: "Many an aching heart found some solace in her gracious smile."

One night at Windsor Castle a crazed deserter, whose family had been killed in an air raid, found his way to the Queen's bedroom and threw himself at her feet, seizing her round the ankles. Queen Elizabeth said

Lady Elizabeth: like one of P.G. Wodehouse's sparky, bubbly, occasionally steely heroines – "Spirited damsels, human ticking bombs".

quietly: "Tell me about it." Later she recalled: "Poor man, I felt so sorry for him. I realised quickly that he did not mean any harm."

Just as she had done during the First World War at Glamis, the Queen kept spirits up at Windsor with charades (Eleanor Roosevelt, America's First Lady, was treated to the spectacle of Queen Elizabeth attired in a false beard for "The Game") and pantomimes starring the now maturing Princesses. Princess Elizabeth joined the ATS in 1944 soon after her 18th birthday and did a course at the Mechanical Transport Training Centre, Aldershot. "We had sparking plugs last night all the way through dinner," complained her proud mother.

After the elation of victory and the celebratory parades, a highlight of the post-war years was the tour of South Africa in 1947. Queen Elizabeth recalled these three-and-a-half months as a particularly happy time – it was effectively the last time "us four" were together as a family before Princess Elizabeth married Prince Philip – though even then King George VI, whose health and temperament were never robust, was showing signs of strain. Angered by the South African nationalists' distaste for the Prime Minister, Field Marshal Smuts, the King exclaimed: "I'd like to shoot them all!" The Queen replied soothingly: "But Bertie, you can't shoot them *all*." Queen Elizabeth's calming, charming influence kept the exhausting show on the road to success. When a disgruntled Afrikaner told her that "we still feel sometimes that we can't forgive the English for conquering us", she replied: "I understand perfectly. We feel very much the same in Scotland." She only tripped up once, when a giant Zulu charged through the police cordon and rushed at the royal party. Queen Elizabeth began belabouring him with her parasol, until she realised that he was offering Princess Elizabeth a 10-shilling note for her 21st birthday. "It was the worst mistake of my life," she said later.

In 1948 the King and Queen celebrated their Silver Wedding anniversary. "Looking back over the last 25 years," she said in a radio broadcast, "and to my own happy childhood I realise more and more the wonderful sense of security and happiness which comes from a loved home." Later that year her first grandchild, Prince Charles, was born, but by this time the King's health was in sharp decline.

The death in 1952 of the husband she had nurtured and moulded into a strong King was a shattering blow to the Queen Mother (as she now became). Stoic as she appeared in public, widowhood proved a much greater strain than many of her cheering admirers appreciated. She took a considerable time to recover from the shock of finding herself a widow at the age of 51. On one occasion she even sought consolation in clairvoyance. A medium, one Lilian Bailey, was invited to Clarence House (the Queen Mother's new home) to conduct a seance at which it was hoped to communicate with the dead King.

Thanking Edith Sitwell for an anthology of poems that had comforted her, the Queen Mother referred to "a day when one felt engulfed by great black clouds of unhappiness and misery". Sorrow, she said "bangs one about until one is senseless". But like the great trouper she has always been, the Queen Mother managed to find a new purpose in a supporting role to her elder daughter, the Queen. "My only wish," she declared, "is that I may be allowed to continue the work that we [*i.e.* the late King and herself] sought to do together." Soon she was undertaking major tours overseas as well as a ceaseless round of engagements at home for the 300-odd organisations of which she had become patron or president.

"Retirement" was never an option. When one of the long-serving ladies-in-waiting at Clarence House suggested that she was too old for the job, the Queen Mother replied: "What about me?"

Above all, Her Majesty was a born survivor. "I shall not go down like the others," she said of her revolver practice during the Second World War. Her expressed determination to live to receive a telegram greeting from her elder daughter on her 100th birthday speaks volumes.

The survival instinct, second nature to the aristocrat, is not always attractive. George Orwell complained that P.G. Wodehouse made the

1920

Lady Elizabeth, who had "come out" as a debutante in the previous Season, begins to make her mark in London Society. This year her parents take a house in Bruton Street, Mayfair, and she strikes up a friendship with her old children's party companion, Prince Albert (newly created Duke of York). They are seen dancing together at the Royal Air Force Ball at the Ritz Hotel. Later in the summer, the Strathmores invite the Duke of York over to Glamis from Balmoral, the Royal Family's castle in Aberdeenshire.

upper classes appear more pleasant than they really are. The Queen Mother herself has been quoted as saying: "You think I am a nice person. I'm not really a nice person." This remark was apparently made in connection with Her Majesty's implacable hostility to the Duchess of Windsor. The refusal to grant the Duchess the style of "Her Royal Highness" was, as it happens, legally and morally indefensible. But Queen Elizabeth's overriding concern was the protection of her husband, King George VI, and the survival of the Monarchy.

Whispering churls have been heard to claim that the Queen Mother has always had a knack of keeping out of trouble, of distancing herself from disagreeable realities. To an outsider it might well seem that she might have done more to steer Princess Margaret during the badly bungled Establishment "waiting game" over her relationship with the war hero Group Captain Peter Townsend, who had become, after all, virtually an adopted son of King George VI and helped withstand many of his rages. And it is regrettable that the Queen Mother could not have offered more guidance to Diana Princess of Wales, an Earl's daughter like herself thrust into the limelight at an even more tender age. But though Lady Diana Spencer set off from under the Queen Mother's roof at Clarence House (where her own grandmother, Ruth Lady Fermoy, was a lady-in-waiting) for her ill-fated wedding to the Prince of Wales in 1981, the two were never especially close.

One also sometimes hears criticism of the Queen Mother blithely ignoring others' illnesses, though in fact she has had more than her fair share of ill health herself. But this, again, is an aspect of her old-fashioned aristocratic toughness – a quality, not always amiable, which rigorously excludes sentimentality and sloppiness from the business, or indeed pleasure, of the day.

The Queen Mother has always been a prime exponent of the philosophy that living well is the best revenge. In between elegant lunches and dinners Her Majesty and her devoted "knitting circle" of long-serving ladies-in-waiting and equerries liked to tuck into the sort of lavish teas – sandwiches, smoked salmon, cream cakes – that one might imagine had disappeared in 1914. Yet there was plenty of work as well as play and, considering what she had done for Britain, the Empire and the Commonwealth, not to mention the House of Windsor, why shouldn't the "Queen Mum" be – well, extravagant, dress in extraordinarily lurid hues (E.M. Forster once claimed he had mistaken her for a wedding-cake), back the odd nag, be a little tardy in paying her bills and procrastinate generally, enjoy a stiffish tincture or twain, see off a few cigarette-burnt eiderdowns, get outside a few dozen chocolate violet creams and generally savour the good things of life?

The reality of Queen Elizabeth is much sharper, more acute, brittle and sophisticated than the popular picture of "the Queen Mum". While at heart a countrywoman, she showed a genuine sympathy for the Arts, and took pleasure in the company of creative people – which gives the lie to the label of Philistine. Those who conjure up an image of her, say, doing a knees-up with Mr Bruce Forsyth, might care to ponder her discerning collection of modern paintings. Works by Sickert, Augustus John, Duncan Grant, Paul Nash, John Piper, Graham Sutherland and John Bratby can be found among the more expected Seagos and Munningses.

All too often hackneyed sugary platitudes – how radiant she is, how gracious and so forth – are trotted out in connection with "the Queen Mum". But Queen Elizabeth is really much more interesting than that, and deserves to be treated more intelligently. Her Majesty has been truly and rightly loved, though real love should embrace the faults as well as the virtues.

While not forgetting her deep religious faith, we are not opening the case for her canonisation here. We are celebrating the life of the 20th century's most charming survivor – Her Majesty Queen Elizabeth The Queen Mother.

FROM DUCHESS TO QUEEN

1921 – 1938

1921

Lady Elizabeth, in the year that she came of age, with her father, Lord Strathmore, honorary Colonel of the 4th/5th Battalion, The Black Watch – the family regiment, in which four of Lady Elizabeth's brothers had served in the Great War, one (Fergus) being killed, the other three all being wounded.

1922

OPPOSITE: *Lady Elizabeth in the year that she became a national celebrity, as a bridesmaid to her Girl Guiding friend Princess Mary (later The Princess Royal) at her marriage to Viscount Lascelles (later 6th Earl of Harewood) at Westminster Abbey – the first of the modern-style "Royal Weddings" that enraptured the press and public. Lady Elizabeth's own possible betrothal to the Duke of York was the subject of much speculation; it was rumoured that she twice turned him down, though in later life The Queen Mother denied this story.*

1923

The wedding group at
Buckingham Palace,
April 26 1923, following
the marriage of the
Duke of York to Lady
Elizabeth Bowes-Lyon at
Westminster Abbey.
From left to right: Lord
Strathmore (wearing the
sash of a Knight Grand
Cross of the Royal
Victorian Order, with
which he had been
invested that morning);
Lady Strathmore; the
Bride (who had caused a
sensation by placing her
bridal bouquet, of white
roses and heather, on the
tomb of the Unknown
Warrior at the Abbey);
the Bridegroom (in RAF
uniform); Queen Mary;
and King George V.
As a consequence of the
ceremony, Lady
Elizabeth Bowes-Lyon
was instantly
transformed into Her
Royal Highness The
Duchess of York, fourth
lady in the land, after
Queen Mary, Queen
Alexandra (King Edward
VII's widow, who lived
on until 1925) and
Princess Mary.
Westminster Abbey had
vetoed the idea of
broadcasting the
marriage service on the
wireless for fear that
men might listen to the
sacrament in public
houses with their
hats on.

1924

The Duchess of York, at a charity fête in London, visits the stall run by the actress Gladys Cooper (40 years later to play Professor Higgins's mother in the film of My Fair Lady*). This summer the Yorks visit Northern Ireland. "Elizabeth has been marvellous as usual and the people simply love her already," reports the Duke to his father. "I am very lucky indeed to have her to help me as she knows exactly what to do and say to all the people we meet."*

1925

OPPOSITE: *The Duke and Duchess of York carried along by a cable-car in the guise of a goose at the British Empire Exhibition, Wembley, which King George V had opened the previous year, when he made his first broadcast on the wireless.*

1926

OPPOSITE: *The Duke and Duchess of York with their baby daughter, Princess Elizabeth, born on April 21 1926 at the Strathmores' London house, No.17 Bruton Street, Mayfair. A "certain line of treatment" (in other words, a Caesarean section) is applied to the Duchess. "The Empire's Little Princess", as the newspapers dub the infant, is the King's first granddaughter and becomes third in line to the throne, following the bachelor Prince of Wales (later Edward VIII) and the Duke of York. "We are so anxious for her first name to be Elizabeth," pleaded the Duke to his father, "as it is such a nice name & there has been no one of that name in your family for a long time..."*

1927

The Duchess of York, an indomitable fisherwoman for almost all her long life, after landing a salmon in New Zealand during her six-month tour of the Empire with the Duke. The infant Princess Elizabeth was left behind. "I felt very much leaving...", the Duchess wrote to Queen Mary, "and the baby was so sweet playing with the buttons on Bertie's uniform that it quite broke me up."

1928

The Duchess of York was constantly active on behalf of her special charities such as the YWCA and the NSPCC and undertook a wide range of public visits. Here she and the Duke are visiting the Browning Settlement in the East End of London where she has always been an immensely popular figure. Indeed she was "crowned" by pearly kings and queens this year at the Costermongers' Annual Ball.

1929

The Duke and Duchess of York, with other members of the Royal Family, at the Highland Games, Braemar. In the spring the Duchess of York had taken the young Princess down to Bognor to cheer up King George V during his convalescence.

1930

OPPOSITE: *The Duchess with her second daughter, Princess Margaret, born at Glamis on August 21 1930 – the first Royal birth to take place in Scotland since 1602, and also the last occasion that the Home Secretary has to be present for the delivery (traditionally to prevent baby-swapping).*

1931

"Us Four", as the Duke of York liked to refer to his family: himself, Princess Elizabeth, the Duchess and Princess Margaret (or "Margaret Rose" as the press delighted in calling her). In this year the Yorks acquired a house in the country, Royal Lodge, in Windsor Great Park. Formerly a cottage orné of the Prince Regent, it had latterly been a "grace and favour" residence for members of the Royal Household. It was to become the cherished weekend retreat of "Us Four".

1932

The Duchess of York chats to the dashing lady racing-driver Mrs Wisdom at the Brooklands circuit in Surrey, a fashionable motor-racing track of the inter-war years.

1933

The Duchess of York is shown a Davy lamp by a Welsh miner at the Abercynon Colliery on her midsummer tour of Wales. It was also in this year that she acquired "Dookie", a Pembroke corgi puppy, the first of the Royal Family's ferocious Welsh breed hailing from the west of the Principality.

1934

ABOVE: *"Sing as we go..." There is a touch of Gracie Fields about this vision of the Duchess of York being cheered along during a tour of a Sheffield steelworks.*

1935

With a characteristic gesture, the Duchess of York tickles the tummy of a baby, little Ann Smith (where is she now?), at a garden party held at St James's Palace in aid of the National Council for Child Welfare. This year King George V and Queen Mary celebrate their Silver Jubilee; the Duke and Duchess of York ride in an open landau to the Thanksgiving Service at St Paul's Cathedral.

1936

In the "Year of the Three Kings", which began with the death of King George V, the Duke and Duchess of York pose on board the Royal Yacht Victoria & Albert *at Cowes in August. It is the calm before the storm. Soon afterwards, the Duchess is shocked to find Mrs Simpson, the new King Edward VIII's twice-divorced American mistress, presiding over a house-party at Balmoral. In December, Edward VIII abdicates the throne; the Royal Family gathers for a grisly dinner-party after the historic Abdication broadcast. "That last family dinner-party was too awful," the new Queen Elizabeth subsequently recalls. "Thank goodness I had 'flu and couldn't go."*

Coronation Day, May 12:
*the new Royal Family
making one of their five
appearances on the
balcony of Buckingham
Palace after the ceremony
at Westminster Abbey.
Queen Elizabeth – who
lost her voice at the end
of this epic day – wears
the crown of Queen
Consort adorned with the
legendary Koh-i-Noor
diamond. The two little
Princesses wear miniature
gold coronets. They
travelled to the Abbey
with their paternal
grandmother, Queen
Mary (not seen in picture
here), who breaks with
precedent – in order to
show solidarity with the
new dawn of the
Monarchy – by becoming
the first Queen Dowager
to attend a Coronation. It
marks an optimistic day
for the new reign.*

1938

OPPOSITE: *During the State Visit to France this July, Queen Elizabeth, in mourning for her mother Lady Strathmore (who died in June), enchants the Parisians with the chic of her full-length mourning white dresses.*

1939

The last summer of peace: the King and Queen and the two Princesses on holiday in Scotland. The King is taking a ciné-film of one of his special interests – a boys' camp at Abergeldie Castle on the Dee, near Balmoral.

THE WAR YEARS

1939 - 1945

St George's Day, 1941, in the East End of London, celebrated for "taking it". "Are we downhearted?" "No!" is the answer of these redoubtable Cockneys chatting to the King and Queen a few days after one of the worst blitzkriegs of the war; in which some 500 German aircraft dropped about 100,000 bombs in an all-night attack.

The Queen framed in a sandbagged bomb shelter in 1939. "Everybody just did their best," she recalled later of the war effort.

The King and Queen, at the heart of their people during the Blitz, visit South London in 1940 to see some of the bomb damage.

1939

Queen Elizabeth broadcasts to the women of the Empire from Buckingham Palace. Although appointed Commander-in-Chief of the Women's Royal Naval Service, the Auxiliary Territorial Service and the Women's Auxiliary Air Force, on the outbreak of the Second World War, she decides not to wear uniform, as it does not suit her informal style. She takes a special interest in the facilities for evacuated mothers and children. As to the question of the possible evacuation to North America of her own children, the Queen says: "The children could not go without me. I won't leave the King, and of course the King will never leave."

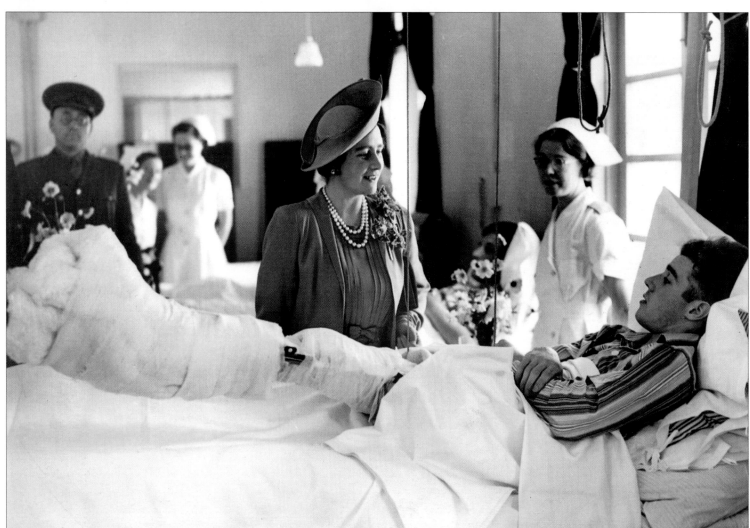

1940

RIGHT: *The Queen inspects Australian soldiers billeted in London at the Victoria League Club.*

BELOW: *The Queen chats to Civil Defence workers in London on another of her stirring Blitz tours.*

BELOW LEFT: *"Many an aching heart," wrote Winston Churchill, "found some solace in her gracious smile": the Queen at the bedside of a wounded "Tommy' in an emergency hospital.*

1940

LEFT: *Buckingham Palace, Friday 13 September: the King and Queen survey the bomb damage to their London home; the chapel has been destroyed.* "I'm glad we've been bombed," *remarks the Queen.* "Now I can look the East End in the face."

1941

ABOVE: *The King and Queen comfort women in Sheffield during a tour of the north. That autumn the Queen's nephew, the Master of Glamis, is killed in action.*

1942

BELOW: *The King and Queen visit Bath, one of the cathedral cities targeted by the Luftwaffe in the so-called "Baedaker Raids". This year, Eleanor Roosevelt, "First Lady" of the USA, comes to stay with the King and Queen at Buckingham Palace and notes the Queen's observation on a tour of Blitzed areas* "that the only solace in the destruction was that new housing would replace the slums."

1942

LEFT: *A rare moment of respite for the King and Queen aboard the destroyer* Bicester, *which brought them back from a tour of Northern Ireland, where Belfast had been badly bombed. In August, the King's youngest surviving brother, the Duke of Kent, is killed on active service in a flying accident in Scotland.*

1944

ABOVE: *The Queen bolsters the morale of the Land Girls on a tour of Berkshire, near her wartime base of Windsor Castle. Her own elder daughter, Princess Elizabeth, joined the ATS this year. "We had sparking plugs last night all the way through dinner," complains her proud mother.*

1940

RIGHT: *The King and Queen have "a cuppa" at a mobile canteen during a tour of Civil Defence centres on Clydeside in Scotland.*

"Digging for Victory": the Queen visits a market garden in Bethnal Green, East London in 1943. This year she acts as a Counsellor of State while King George VI flies secretly to North Africa to see his troops. The aircraft is re-routed due to fog at Gibraltar.

"Of course," the Queen writes to Queen Mary (who is spending the war at Badminton in Gloucestershire, enthusiastically contributing to the rural war effort), "I imagined every sort of horror, and walked up and down my room staring at the telephone."

1945

ABOVE: *"Gawd, bless yer, Ma'am!" The East End cheers the King and Queen as the long war grinds to a halt at last.*

OPPOSITE: *"Smile by your bunks..." The Queen visits an underground shelter dormitory for young South Londoners.*

1944

RIGHT: *"Over here..." The King and Queen visit a United States airbase in the run-up to D-Day on June 6, when the Allies began the invasion of occupied Europe.*

1945

*"We want the King!"
chanted the crowds on
VE-Day, May 8 1945,
outside Buckingham
Palace. "We want the
Queen!" The King and
Queen, together with the
Prime Minister, Winston
Churchill, and the two
Princesses, Elizabeth in
ATS uniform and
Margaret, acknowledge
the cheers of the multitude
from the balcony. Later
the two Princesses
themselves slip away into
the throng below (and to
join in the chanting for
the King
and Queen). The Queen
prepares sandwiches for
the return of the two
teenagers. "Poor darlings,"
notes the King in his
diary, "they have never
had any fun yet."*

PEACE COMES

1946-1959

1946

Conversation Piece: one of the last studies (albeit rather stilted and overly formal) of "Us Four". Soon it was to be five, with Princess Elizabeth becoming unofficially engaged to Prince Philip that August.

1947
Swazi salute: the King and Queen and Princess Elizabeth at a rally of 4,000 Swazi warriors at Goedegun during their four-month tour of Southern Africa. Unfortunately, on another occasion, when one giant Zulu charges through the police cordon and rushes at the Royal party, Queen Elizabeth begins to belabour him with her parasol before realising he is offering Princess Elizabeth a 10-shilling note as a 21st birthday present. "It was the worst mistake of my life," she says later.

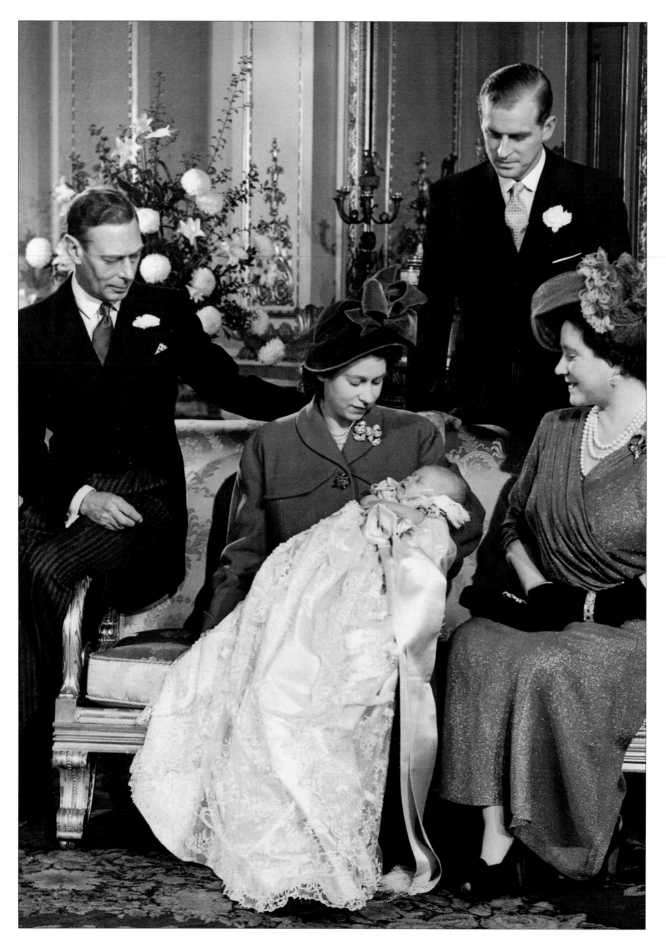

1948

OPPOSITE: *In the year of her Silver Wedding anniversary ("I realise more and more the wonderful sense of security and happiness which comes from a loved home," she says in a broadcast to the nation), the King and Queen attend the christening of their first grandchild, Prince*

Charles, in the Music Room at Buckingham Palace on December 15 1948. The month-old Prince, to whom his grandmother is always specially close, wears the Royal Christening Robe of white silk and Honiton lace first made for Queen Victoria's children.

1949

The King and Queen drive down the course at Ascot on the first day of the Royal Meeting in an open landau with the Duke of Gloucester (left) and the Duke of Beaufort, Master of the Horse. The previous Saturday the King, by now a sick man, had been obliged

to take the salute at the Birthday Parade (Trooping the Colour) from his carriage on Horse Guards Parade. He had been operated on for arterial sclerosis in March.

1950

Queen Elizabeth attempts to recapture the fleeing Prince Charles for the photographer at the christening of his sister, Princess Anne, in the Music Room at Buckingham Palace. Princess Elizabeth holds the baby, born at Clarence House (then the London home of the Princess and her husband, the Duke of Edinburgh) on August 15 1950. This year the Queen celebrates her half-century.

1951

The Queen, in feathered
headgear, attends an
educational garden party in
the grounds of Westminster
Abbey. In May of this year
the King and Queen declare
the Festival of Britain open
– it is to be the last major
public appearance for the
King, who is now afflicted
with lung cancer.

1952

OPPOSITE: *The three
grieving Queens – Queen
Elizabeth II, Queen Mary
and Queen Elizabeth The
Queen Mother (as she is
now to be styled) – at the
Lying-in-State of King
George VI at Westminster
Hall. The King had died at
Sandringham, the Royal
Family's Norfolk estate, on*
6 February, whereupon the
new Queen, Elizabeth II,
returned from the tour of
Africa she had been
undertaking on his behalf.
After the King's funeral at
St George's Chapel,
Windsor, the Queen
Mother, grief-stricken,
repairs to Birkhall, on the
Balmoral estate.

1953

The Queen Mother's procession in Westminster Abbey for the Coronation of Queen Elizabeth II, on June 2 1953. Preceding her is her personal Lord Chamberlain, the 12th Earl of Airlie (whose second son, Angus Ogilvy, was to marry Princess Alexandra of Kent). Behind follows the procession of Princess Margaret. The Queen Mother has taken her grandson, Prince Charles, in the Glass Coach to the Abbey to see the Queen crowned. Her Majesty watches from the middle of the Royal Gallery. The previous month she had moved into Clarence House.

1954

The Queen Mother presents the FA Cup to the captain of the winning team, West Bromwich Albion, at Wembley. Following her husband's death, Winston Churchill, the Prime Minister, had felt compelled to see her in order to encourage her to play a new role in public life as "the Queen Mother" (a title previously used for Queen Dowagers but one she emphatically made her own). She rose magnificently to the challenge.

1955

The Queen Mother at the Castle of Mey (formerly known as Barrogill Castle), in Caithness, which she had first seen when staying with her friends the Vyners in the summer after the King's death. Remote and threatened with demolition, the castle appealed to the romantic nature of the Queen Mother, who determined to save it. Restored and adorned with a notable garden, the renamed Castle of Mey became a much loved, if windy, retreat.

1956

OPPOSITE: *The Queen Mother descends the steps of a traditional Romany caravan in the gardens of Marlborough House at the "Horse to Helicopter" fair in aid of the Royal College of Nursing. This year she becomes the first member of the Royal Family to use a helicopter for getting about. "The chopper," she quips, "has changed my life – as it did that of Anne Boleyn" (the previous mother of a reigning Queen).*

1957

Complete with miner's helmet, the Queen Mother prepares to go down a copper mine in Northern Rhodesia during her African tour in the summer.

1958

OPPOSITE: *During her
world tour – in which
she became the first
member of the Royal
Family to fly round the
globe – the indefatigable
Queen Mother
acknowledges the cheers
of 30,000 schoolchildren
at the Brisbane Oval
in Australia.*

1959

*Back home at
Sandringham, the Queen
Mother has a kindly
word with young tent-
crashers at the Royal
Norfolk Agricultural
Show during a warm
summer. Princess
Margaret (with whom
the Queen Mother had
earlier that year had an
audience with Pope John
in Rome and lunched
with General de Gaulle
in Paris) looks on. She
was to marry the photog-
rapher Antony
Armstrong-Jones (later
Earl of Snowdon) the
next year.*

1939

LEFT: *The King and Queen acknowledge the salute of the royal jockey Gordon Richards (later knighted) before he goes to mount the King's filly Great Truth at Sandown Park in the last summer of peace. It finished third.*

1964

ABOVE: *The Queen Mother enjoys a "treble" (three winners) at Folkestone races.*

1974

BELOW: *The Queen Mother, with the Queen, walking the cross-country course at the Badminton Horse Trials.*

1969

ABOVE: *The Queen Mother presents a souvenir trophy to the ever-cheerful former champion National Hunt jockey Terry Biddlecombe after he has won the Mackeson Gold Cup at Cheltenham on Gay Trip. Biddlecombe will subsequently ride for the Queen Mother and her trainer Fulke Walwyn.*

1996

TOP RIGHT: *A suitably continental gesture from the flamboyant jockey "Frankie" Dettori as the Queen Mother presents the trophy to the leading rider at the Royal Meeting at Ascot.*

1986

BELOW: *The Queen Mother in the winners' enclosure at Sandown with her horse Insular (triumphant in the Imperial Cup) and her trainer Ian Balding. It is her second winner of the day.*

1986

RIGHT: *The Queen Mother, escorted by the Prince of Wales, makes her way through the crowds in the Royal Enclosure at Ascot during the Royal Meeting. The manager of the Royal Studs at Sandringham, Michael Oswald, brings up the rear.*

1956

MIDDLE LEFT: *The Queen Mother, first lady of steeplechasing, in the paddock with (to the left) her trainer Peter Cazalet and (to the right of Princess Margaret) jockey Dick Francis. He was riding Devon Loch to what looked like a certain victory in the 1956 Grand National when, yards from the finish, the horse unbelievably collapsed. "I must go down and comfort those poor people," says the Queen Mother in her box at Aintree, later observing philosophically, "That's racing."*

1997

LEFT: *The Queen Mother with her winning jockey, Major Oliver Ellwood, after her horse Norman Conqueror has won the Royal Artillery Cup at Sandown.*

INTO THE SIXTIES

1960 - 1976

1960

OPPOSITE: *After a decade's gap, another grandchild for the Queen Mother – Prince Andrew, born February 19 1960. The next month she distributes the Royal Maundy at Westminster Abbey for the first time. "I had no idea," she says, "that the service was so long."*

1961

The Queen Mother's annual tribute to the Fallen: she plants a cross in the British Legion Field of Remembrance at St Margaret's Westminster on the eve of Armistice Day, November 11. A week earlier she acquired a fourth grandchild when Princess Margaret,

Countess of Snowdon, gave birth to a son, David, styled Viscount Linley. In the summer the Queen Mother broke a bone in her foot, but, nothing daunted, she was wheeled on to the Vickers-Armstrong platform at Tyneside to launch the liner Northern Star.

1962

The Queen Mother has been a constant visitor to Northern Ireland in fair weather and foul. This spring she attended a ceremony at Queen's University, Belfast, from which she had received an honorary Doctorate of Laws back in 1924.

1963

OPPOSITE: *Her Majesty at 63 in the drawing room at Clarence House. She wears a gold embroidered dress with wheatear motif adorned with Garter sash and Star together with the Royal Family Orders of her husband and her elder daughter. This year she began her annual custom of visiting French chateaux on the Loire.*

1964

OPPOSITE: *"Hold on to your hat": back from convalescing in the Caribbean after an appendix operation, the Queen Mother tours gardens in Lewisham on behalf of the London Gardens Society. Two more grandchildren, Prince Edward and Lady Sarah Armstrong-Jones, are born.*

1965

The Queen Mother, together with Princess Margaret and Lord Snowdon, attends the service to mark the 900th anniversary of the consecration of Westminster Abbey. This year sees the deaths of Sir Winston Churchill and the Princess Royal. In the summer the Queen Mother invites her friend Noel Coward to stay at Sandringham, where they sing the music-hall ditty "My Old Man Said Follow The Van".

1966

The wader-clad Queen Mother fishing in the Dee the year she underwent what was officially described as "a serious abdominal operation" (said to be a colostomy) at the King Edward V11 Hospital for officers ("Sister Agnes's") in London.

1967

The Royal Family are seen in public together with the Duke and Duchess of Windsor (the former Edward VIII and Mrs Simpson) for the first time. The occasion is the unveiling of a memorial plaque to Queen Mary at Marlborough House. Front row (left to right): Prince Philip, the Queen, the Queen Mother, the Duke and Duchess of Gloucester and the Duke and Duchess of Windsor.

1968

The Queen Mother walks
in the Garter procession
with her grandson, the
Prince of Wales, at Windsor
where he is invested and
installed as a Knight of this
Most Noble Order of
Chivalry (founded by King
Edward III in 1348). The
Prince, denied the Eton
education his wise
grandmother wanted for
him, is now blossoming as
an undergraduate at
Cambridge and will be
invested as Prince of
Wales at Caernarvon Castle
the next year.

1969

"It's a long way to Tipperary..." The Queen Mother inspects Chelsea Pensioners from the Royal Hospital at the British Legion Field of Remembrance.

1970

OPPOSITE: *A study in pearls by Cecil Beaton to mark the Queen Mother's 70th birthday.*

1971

The Queen Mother at the Royal Opera House, Covent Garden, with (right) the Duchess of Kent and (left) the then Prime Minister, Edward Heath. Her Majesty became a fervent admirer of Heath's successor as Leader of the Conservative Party, Margaret Thatcher.

1972

The Queen Mother presides over a gathering of the Queen's Institute of District Nursing at St James's Palace. The corgi of unreliable aspect in the foreground is Blackie.

To the left is her sister-in-law the Duchess of Gloucester, who lost her elder son, Prince William, in a flying accident this year. He once paid this tribute to the

Queen Mother: "I can't tell you what the Queen Mother means to all of us. You only have to be loved by her – and to love her yourself – to know that, no matter what,

you could never let her down." This year also saw the death of the Duke of Windsor in Paris and the Silver Wedding of the Queen and Prince Philip.

1973

A feather in her cap, the Queen Mother attends the North of Scotland Gun Dog Association Retriever Trials on the Balmoral estate. That winter, Princess Anne married her fellow equestrian, Captain Mark Phillips, at Westminster Abbey.

1974

OPPOSITE TOP: *Watching the Highland Games at Braemar from the comparative comfort of the Royal Box are (front row, from left to right): Queen Anne-Marie of The Hellenes, the Queen, Prince Edward, the Queen Mother and King Constantine of The Hellenes. The prominent figure in the second row, to the left of Prince Edward, is the Duke of Fife, great-grandson of King Edward VII.*

1975

OPPOSITE BELOW: *The Queen Mother celebrates her 75th birthday with two of her devoted grandsons, the Prince of Wales and Prince Andrew – who has presented her with a pair of pottery dishes he has made at Gordonstoun School. The occasion is also marked by a special composition by Benjamin Britten.*

1976

The "see-through" umbrella has long been a standard prop for the Queen Mother, though it was not much needed in the summer, which was notably hot. Princess Margaret and Lord Snowdon separated in the spring.

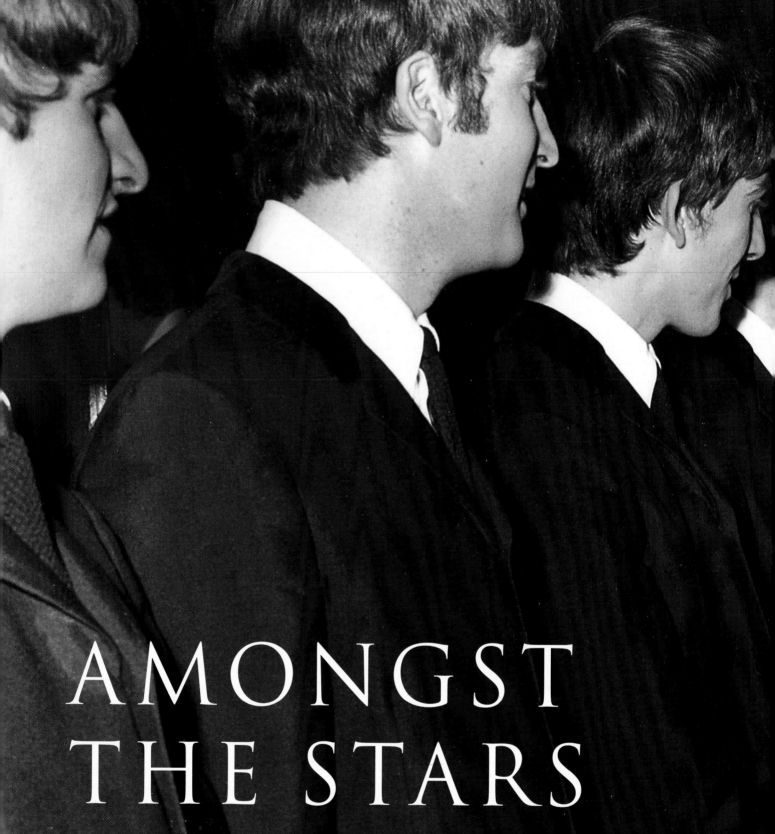

AMONGST THE STARS

1963
*"Beatlemania" enlivens
the Royal Variety show
at the London
Palladium.*

1968

TOP: *"Stop! In the name of love…" The Supremes are presented to the Queen Mother. Frankie Howerd awaits his moment.*

1972

LEFT: *Three veteran troupers share the proverbial joke: the Queen Mother, comedian Ken Dodd and female impersonator Danny La Rue.*

1961

ABOVE: *The Queen Mother shakes hands with Adam Faith at the Royal Variety Performance. Max Bygraves beams beside.*

1966

ABOVE: *"Is there an answer to that?" The Queen Mother tangles with Morecambe and Wise.*

1970

RIGHT: *The ubiquitous Bygraves sandwiched between the American singers Dionne Warwick and Andy Williams as the Queen Mother works the line at the Palladium.*

1963

BELOW: *Not to be outdone by the Beatles, Marlene Dietrich chats to the Queen Mother at the 1963 Royal Variety Performance. Michael Flanders looks up from his wheelchair.*

THE SILVER JUBILEE AND BEYOND

1977-1999

1978

ABOVE: *A 78th birthday wave from the Queen Mother outside Clarence House – a regular place of pilgrimage on August 4.*

1977

OPPOSITE: *The Queen Mother's first great-grandchild, Peter Phillips, is christened at Buckingham Palace in the Queen's Silver Jubilee year. Princess Anne holds the baby.*

1979

The Queen Mother is installed as the 160th Lord Warden of the Cinque Ports and Constable of Dover Castle – the first lady to hold this historic post – in August. She tells those attending the ceremony that she has the right to the "fishes royal", though has to pay for the burial of stranded whales. Later that month, Lord Mountbatten is murdered at Mullaghmore by Irish terrorists.

1980

PREVIOUS PAGE: *The joyful celebrations of the Queen Mother's 80th birthday dominated the year. There were special garden-parties at Holyroodhouse in Edinburgh and Buckingham Palace (with guest lists drawn from the 300-odd organisations over which she presided); a regimental tribute at the Royal Tournament; a Covent Garden gala specially choreographed by her friend Sir Frederick Ashton; and a Thanksgiving Service at St Paul's Cathedral where the Queen yielded precedence to her mother, complete with Sovereign's Escort of Household Cavalry. The flamboyantly-coiffed figure behind is the Queen Mother's faithful stalwart at Clarence House, William Tallon.*

1981

The fairy-tale scene on the balcony at Buckingham Palace after the wedding of the Prince and Princess of Wales, July 26. The Queen Mother and the Queen are both in blue; the bridegroom, Prince Philip and the two pages (Lord Nicholas Windsor, younger son of the Duke of Kent, and Edward van Cutsem) are all in naval uniform; Prince Edward, on the right, in morning dress. The three young bridesmaids, in Victorian-style dresses and garlands, are Sarah Jane Gaselee, Catherine Cameron and Clementine Hambro – whose great-grandfather, Winston Churchill, had taken his place on the same balcony for the VE-Day celebrations in 1945.

1982

OPPOSITE: *The Queen Mother at the State Banquet for the Sultan of Oman at Buckingham Palace on St Patrick's Day. The next month she visits Northern Ireland for the first time since the modern "Troubles" began in 1969. Also in this year, her grandson, Prince Andrew, serves in the Falklands war; the Princess of Wales gives birth to Prince William; and in November, the Queen Mother undergoes an operation to remove a fishbone that has become lodged in her throat. She has resumed her ceaseless round of royal duties by the end of the month.*

1983

The Queen Mother chats to a member of the Parachute Regiment among a guard of honour at the Royal Tournament, at Earls Court.

1984

In support of the British "Venice in Peril" Fund, the Queen Mother fulfils a long-held ambition to see Venice. Accompanied by the captain of the Royal Yacht Britannia, Rear-Admiral Paul Greening, she laughs off the gift of "Just one Cornetto" (a popular ice-cream advertising slogan of the day) from a publicity-conscious gondolier, though it is not clear whether she quite understands the joke. In the Queen's Christmas broadcast that year there is film of the Queen Mother at the recent christening of Prince Harry of Wales. "I really believe he is going to smile," says the proud great-grandmother.

1985

*Norman Parkinson's
85th birthday study of
the Queen Mother and
four of her grandchildren
at Windsor Castle: the
Prince of Wales, Prince
Edward, Princess Anne
and Prince Andrew.*

1986

The July wedding of Prince Andrew (newly created Duke of York) to Sarah Ferguson, daughter of a polo-playing friend of Prince Philip, at Westminster Abbey. From left to right: Princess Anne (soon to be created Princess Royal); the Duchess of Kent; the Princess of Wales; the Duke of Kent; the Prince of Wales; the Queen Mother; the Duchess of Gloucester; Prince Philip; the Queen; the Duke of Gloucester and Princess Alice, Duchess of Gloucester. In the spring the Queen Mother had attended the funeral of the Duchess of Windsor (denied the style of "Royal Highness" in death as in life) at Windsor.

1987

OPPOSITE: *A pint for the publicist's dream: the Queen Mother tactfully samples a glass of bitter ("It's very nice") at the Queen's Head pub in Stepney on a visit to the East End of London in connection with the London Gardens Society. This picture still adorns every Youngs public house in the land.*

1988

The Queen Mother greets a new recruit to "the Met", the young foal Quince, at the Brixton Police Stables. She had visited the area a few years earlier after rioting in the streets.

1989

Mounties and maple-leafs: the Queen Mother in Canada, 50 years after her triumphant pre-war tour of 1939.

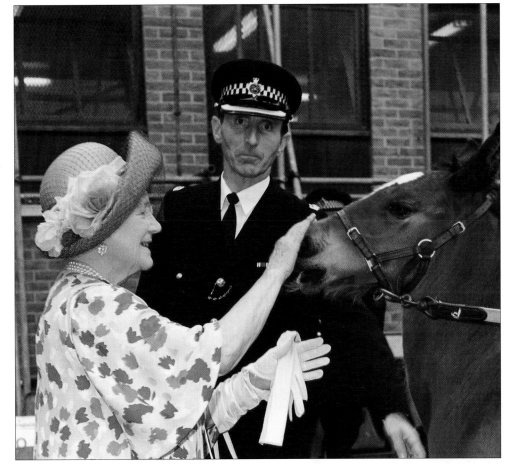

1990

The Queen Mother and the Princess of Wales share a landau at Ascot for the Royal Meeting. The Princess was a granddaughter of two of Her Majesty's ladies-in-waiting and a great-niece of four more – but how close were they really?

1992

OPPOSITE: *The Queen Mother still wearing her poppy with pride. As the years passed she became the icon of Remembrance. This year she braved controversy by unveiling the memorial statue of Marshal of the RAF Sir Arthur "Bomber" Harris in the Strand.*

1991

Old soldiers never die: the Queen Mother at the Royal Hospital, Chelsea. Far from fading away herself, she carried out 102 official engagements in this year alone.

1993

*"By the left, quick march..."
The Queen Mother, now
with a walking stick, on
parade in Hounslow to
present new colours to the
King's Regiment.*

1995

OPPOSITE: *The Queen
Mother leaves Sister Agnes's
in November after
successfully undergoing an
operation to replace her
right hip. Her faithful
private secretary and
equerry, Sir Alastair Aird,
follows behind.*

1994

*The Queen Mother meets
veterans of the D-Day
Landings in Normandy
50 years before on a trip
organised by the London*
*Taxi Benevolent Association
for War Disabled. Forever
the "Forces Sweetheart", the
singer Dame Vera Lynn
looks on.*

1996

Shamrocks on parade for St Patrick's Day: the Queen Mother with officers and men of the Irish Guards.

1997

The Queen Mother greets her great-granddaughters Princess Beatrice and Eugenie, together with their father, the Duke of York, at Scrabster, in Caithness, near the Castle of Mey.

1998

ABOVE: *Happy scenes outside Clarence House on the Queen Mother's 98th birthday: she is seen with (left to right) the Prince of Wales, Prince William, Zara Phillips and Prince Harry.*

1999

RIGHT: *The Queen Mother is in cheerful mood at Flitcham Church on the morning of Sunday, January 24. But within hours, at Sandringham, she complains of a serious nosebleed and has an operation at the Queen Elizabeth Hospital in King's Lynn. A Clarence House spokesman says later, "She is perfectly all right."*

ABOVE: *A saucy sideways glance in 1989.*
OPPOSITE: *A classic wave during a visit to a hospice in Esher in 1996.*
ENDPAPER: *Norman Parkinson's "Royal Blue Trinity" study for the Queen Mother's 80th birthday. This portrait of Her Majesty with her two daughters, the Queen and Princess Margaret was likened to a publicity still for The Supremes.*

The Daily Telegraph

CREATIVE DIRECTOR: *Clive Crook*
EDITORIAL PROJECTS DIRECTOR: *George Darby*

THE QUEEN MOTHER:
WOMAN OF THE CENTURY

DESIGN: *David Riley*
PICTURE RESEARCH: *Colin Smith*
TEXT: *Hugh Massingberd*
EDITORIAL ASSISTANT: *Olivia Elms*

PICTURE CREDITS:
Hulton Getty: Pages 5 (top left); 17 (bottom right); 18; 23; 28; 29; 31; 32 (top and bottom); 33; 34 (bottom); 35; 36 (top and bottom); 38/39; 40; 42/43; 44; 46 (bottom); 47 (top and bottom); 48/49; 49 (top); 51 (top); 52/53; 55 (top and bottom); 64/65; 66; 67; 68; 71; 73; 75 (top); 76 (top left, centre right, bottom left); 78; 79; 80; 83; 84 (bottom); 86/87; 91; 94/95; 96 (top and bottom left); 97 (bottom left); 98 (left); 100/101; 104; 105; **Camera Press:** Front cover: Endpaper 1; Titlepage; 3; 4 (top left, bottom right); 5 (top right); 12; 15; 21; 26/27; 34 (top); 58/59; 77; 81; 88; 92 (top and bottom); 93; 113 (bottom); 120; back cover. **B.I.P.P.A. (British International Photographic Press Agencies):** page: 96 (bottom right) **Tim Graham:** pages 102/103. **Harris Picture Agency:** page 6 **Metropolitan Police:** page 113 (top) **Sygma/Norman Parkinson:** pages 108/109; 122/123 (endpaper 2): **Rex:** page 114 (top)

Anwar Hussein: page 99 **Press Association:** pages 2; 5 (bottom left); 24; 30; 56; 62; 82; 89; 90; 97 (top); 106/107; 112; **Mirror Syndication:** pages 16/17; 69 (top); **E.O. Hoppe:** page 19; **Popperfoto:** pages 4 (top right); 10/11; 25; 84 (top); **The Daily Telegraph:** pages 37; 41; 45; 46 (top); 50; 51 (bottom); 69 (bottom) **Reg Davis:** pages 4 (bottom left); 75 (bottom left); **Reuters:** pages 5 (bottom left); 118 (top); 121 **Daily Mail:** pages 49 (bottom); 97 (bottom right); **Topical:** page 54; **Associated Press:** pages 56/57; 60/61; 63; **U.P.I.:** pages 74/75; **Ed Byrne:** page 76 (top right) **P.N.A. (Picture News Agencies):** page 85; **Evening Standard:** page 98 (right); **Daily Express:** page 115; **James Fraser:** page 116 (top); **European Photo Agency:** page 116 (bottom); **Brian Smith:** page 117; **James Gray:** page 118 (bottom); **Ian Jones:** page 119 (top); **Alban Donohoe:** page 119 (bottom)